Glen Hansard
GUITAR SONGBOOK

Produced by
Alfred Music Publishing Co., Inc.
P.O. Box 10003
Van Nuys, CA 91410-0003
alfred.com

Printed in USA.

ISBN-10: 0-7390-9398-3
ISBN-13: 978-0-7390-9398-6

Cover photo: David Cleary • Back cover photo and title page photos: Conor Masterson • Page 2: Portrait sketch by Colin Davidson, copyright: the artist.
Album art: *Fitzcarraldo* © 1996 ZTT Records/SALVO • *Dance the Devil...* © 1999 ZTT Records/SALVO
For the Birds © 2001 Plateau Records Ltd./Overcoat Recordings • *The Swell Season* © 2006 Plateau Records Ltd./Overcoat Recordings
Once © 2012 Sony Music Entertainment/Masterworks • *Strict Joy* © 2009 Plateau Records Ltd./ANTI
Rhythm and Repose © 2012 Plateau Records Ltd./ANTI

 Alfred Cares. Contents printed on 100% recycled paper.

Contents

BACK BROKE

*To match recording, Capo II

Moderately ♩ = 128

Intro:

Words and Music by
GLEN HANSARD

*Recording sounds one whole step higher than written.

Back Broke - 3 - 1

Back Broke - 3 - 3

DROWN OUT

Moderately in 2 ♩ = 120

Intro:

Words and Music by
GLEN HANSARD

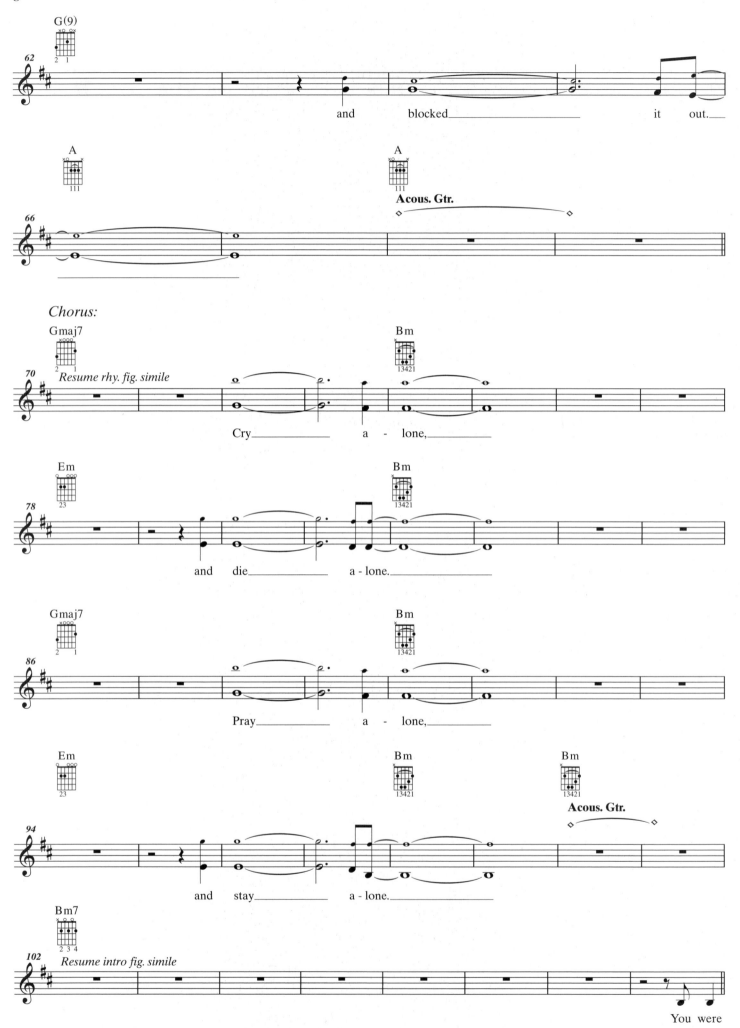

Chorus:

Verse 3:

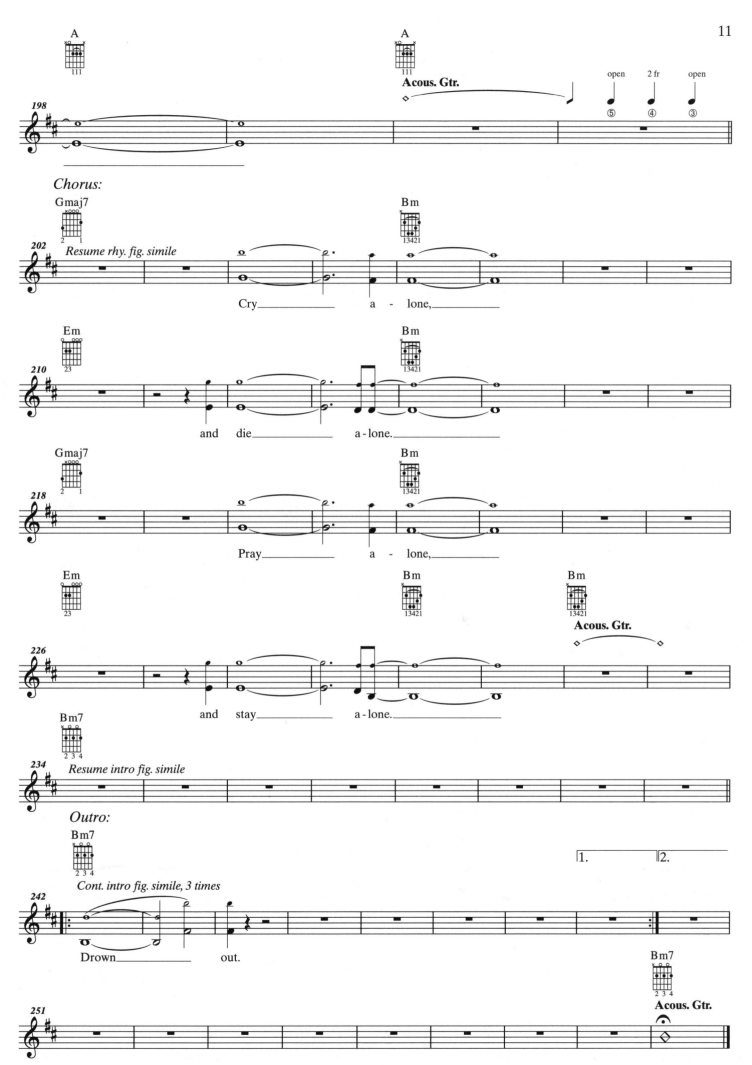

Chorus:

Cry_____ a - lone,_____

and die_____ a - lone.

Pray_____ a - lone,_____

and stay_____ a - lone.

Outro:

Drown_____ out.

FALLING SLOWLY

Words and Music by
GLEN HANSARD and MARKETA IRGLOVA

HIGH HOPE

Words and Music by
GLEN HANSARD

LAY ME DOWN

Words and Music by
GLEN HANSARD and THE FRAMES

Moderately in 2 ♩ = 104

Lay Me Down - 3 - 1

LOVE DON'T LEAVE ME WAITING

*Drop D tuning w/Capo II: ⑥ = D

Moderately ♩ = 106

Words and Music by
GLEN HANSARD

*Recording sounds one whole step higher than written due to capo.
**Chord frames and strum are suggested by Glen Hansard's guitar part in live performances.

Love Don't Leave Me Waiting - 3 - 1

%. *Chorus:*

LOW RISING

Words and Music by
GLEN HANSARD

THE MOON

Words and Music by
GLEN HANSARD

The Moon - 3 - 1

28

*Open 1st, 2nd, & 3rd strings are technically not part Dm, but at times ring out, mirroring Em and Cmaj7 which both have open 1st, 2nd, & 3rd strings.

MAYBE NOT TONIGHT

Words and Music by
GLEN HANSARD

RED CHORD

*To match recording, Capo IV

Words and Music by
GLEN HANSARD and THE FRAMES

Moderately slow ♩ = 74

Intro:

*Recording sounds two whole steps higher than written.

And I'm pull-ing on the

Chorus:

red chord   that pulls you back___ to me,_____ Lord,

that helps me out___   when you're___   a - way._

Red Chord - 5 - 1

Verse 2:

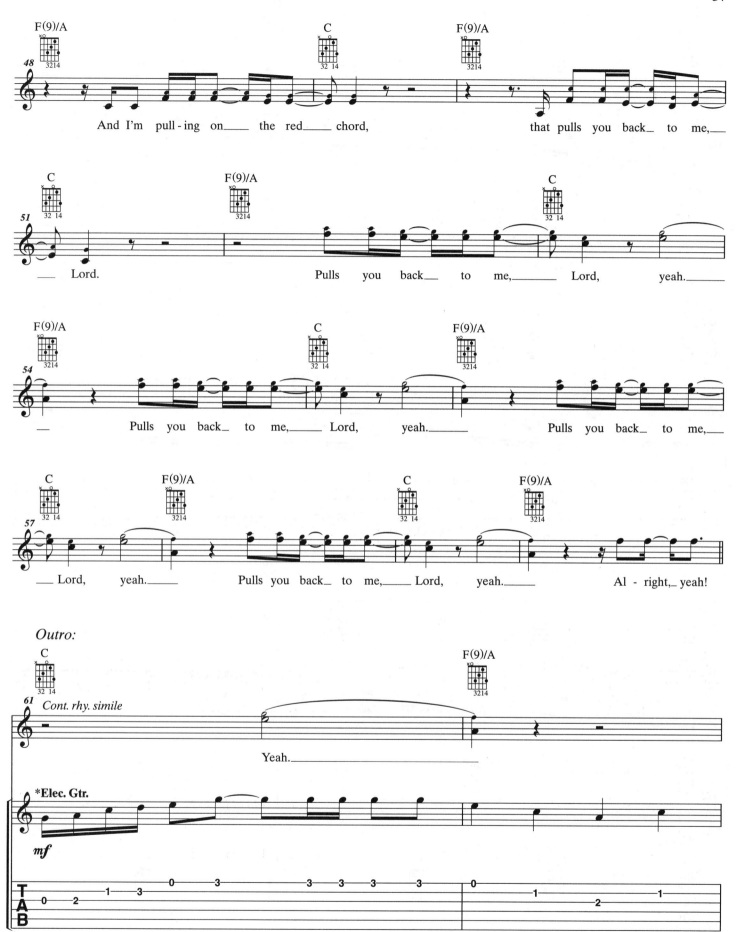

*Elec. Gtr. also w/capo IV (TAB numbers relative to capo).
Elec. Gtr. sounds 8va (one octave higher) on recording.

SONG OF GOOD HOPE

Words and Music by
GLEN HANSARD

*If we're gon-na make__ __ it a-cross this riv-er a-live___ you need to think like a boat__ __ and go with the tide.__ I know where you've been_*

Song of Good Hope - 3 - 1

40

STAR STAR**

Words and Music by
GLEN HANSARD and THE FRAMES

Star Star** - 3 - 1

44

YOU WILL BECOME

Words and Music by
GLEN HANSARD

You Will Become - 3 - 1

TALKING WITH THE WOLVES

Words and Music by
GLEN HANSARD

*Recording sounds one whole step higher than written.
** Chords frames are for reference.

THIS GIFT

*To match recording, Capo I

Moderately slow ♩ = 82

Intro:

Words and Music by
GLEN HANSARD and MARKETA IRGLOVA

*Recording sounds a half step higher than written.

§ Chorus:

This gift will last for-ev-er, this gift will nev-er let you down.__

__ Some things are made from bet-ter stuff, this gift is {wait-ing / read-y} to be found.__

__ Your heart's in wide re-ceiv-ing, been too long bur-ied in__ the sand.__

__ Some things re-quire__ leav-ing, {this gift will / these things just} fall right in your__

This Gift - 4 - 1

WHAT ARE WE GONNA DO

Moderately slow ♩ = 78

Words and Music by
GLEN HANSARD and PADDY CASEY

WHAT HAPPENS WHEN THE HEART JUST STOPS

Words and Music by
GLEN HANSARD and THE FRAMES

Moderately slow ♩ = 76

Intro:

What Happens When the Heart Just Stops - 4 - 1

Bridge:

Chorus 2:

Outro:

Cont. rhy. simile

Elec. Gtr.

hold throughout

What Happens When the Heart Just Stops - 4 - 4

YOUR FACE

Words and Music by
GLEN HANSARD and THE FRAMES

Your Face - 5 - 1

68